In the Land of Opportunity Beware

Carolyn Sabuni

AuthorHouse™ UK
1663 Liberty Drive
Bloomington, IN 47403 USA
www.authorhouse.co.uk
UK TFN: 0800 0148641 (Toll Free inside the UK)
UK Local: 02036 956322 (+44 20 3695 6322 from outside the UK)

Because of the dynamic nature of the Internet, any web addresses or links contained in this book may have changed since publication and may no longer be valid. The views expressed in this work are solely those of the author and do not necessarily reflect the views of the publisher, and the publisher hereby disclaims any responsibility for them.

Any people depicted in stock imagery provided by Getty Images are models, and such images are being used for illustrative purposes only.
Certain stock imagery © Getty Images.

This book is printed on acid-free paper.

ISBN: 978-1-6655-8555-2 (sc)
ISBN: 978-1-6655-8556-9 (e)

Print information available on the last page.

Published by AuthorHouse 02/16/2021

authorHOUSE®

Acknowledgements

Thank you, God. I am thankful for this ride of life and for keeping me going.

Thank you, Mother. You're amazing!

Thank you to everyone who loves me. You're precious, I tell you. And I love you too.

Thank you to my incredible sister.

Thank you, AuthorHouse.

Omar, the first time I wrote poetry was because of you. You brought me to my first poetry group. You saw me before I did. Thank you.

Thank you to all the people I've come across. You've inspired me in every way.

Thank you, reader. I am grateful for your existence.

~You're all capable of anything
you wish to achieve, so fly.~

Contents

Section 1

Creativity is intelligence having fun.

~Albert Einstein

Right

Dark or light?

I might just fight to see which ignites.

In times of night,

I come to face that awkward fright

That I might just be right.

For what I fight

Is my creative delight.

In Tune

The laugh,
The cheer,
Accompanied in their best gear.

Only to discover that it's near, the hollow whispers, the endearing of it.

Hoped it away.
Wished it away.
Pushed it away.

When the dog barks,
The night deemed shallow.

Almost grasping at a chance to touch again,

To be in tune
Admitted

So soulfully
Was whole.

Don't get that again,
That misty air,
That wishful thought.

So time can tell—
So what?

She sat and stared,
A companion bared.

Jail could feel like this.
Alien.

That harmless saying,
"You're only a product of your environment."

She'd hope it would regenerate
Nationwide.
So un a fix.

Misty

I'm provoked with
No evoke.

I handle terrors
With all that's
Spoke.

It minds me.
I just abide.

Though days
Come round,
It's all about peace.

Brother, please come back to this.

I know you'd rather
Be amidst
Of all that's
Bliss.

Even when time
Feels to skip.

I pray you quit
And
Don't what it is
And go live on a cliff.

Actually scratch that
Whatever you finds
Not in the mix.

Prey

With no regret,
My dear.

They all love to appear.

So ego wouldn't be so near.

It is whole
But
Meaningless

They say.

They parade in
all their façade,
And
Hope that one
Day

There would come
A day

Where
They no longer
Felt like prey.

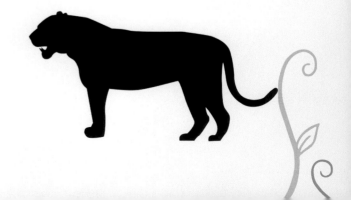

Pest

Youth, youth, youth
And
all its booth.

A move of spite
May cause delight.

Though many cheer,
But watch their peer.

For they do not
Know what is
Near.

It feeds on us
And
You.

It mistreats the sweet
And
Makes them weak.

It holds you on
Monetary value
And
Drives you shallow.

Cautious
And
All will be deeper.

Section 2

If you can dream it, you can do it.

~Walt Disney

Mess

Oh, how divine
A summer's day,
So re-aligned.

I almost fried
At the thought of
Awkward minds.

It wouldn't hurt to make a mess,
To do these things I can't oppress.
But ...

I wouldn't mind
If I just ride along
The wave of seeded
Minds.

So insecure,
So mistaken
And pure.

Oh, Cindy Lou,
You precious thing
To be protected.
Why, oh why
Do they cry
For the poor weep?

The city's cold,
The bars so weak.
They help the wealth.

"Undo it all,"
She said one day.

She couldn't scream,
But all can hear
If hearts are dear.

It wouldn't hurt
To make a mess.
To do these things
They can't oppress.

Adulthood

Adulthood taught her
Not to be nice.

It brings the mood up
On days like these,
The sky not blue.

They all laugh with each other,
But are they really laughing
With each other,
Or do they wish to pass the
Time?

It's only right
I make it out,
And
I'll do all right.

He doesn't care if people judge.
He'd rather be this way below.
Once he's above,
He'll feel himself.

Oh, they envy one another
So much.

Why is that?

He released; he is him,
And nobody can
Take that
Except she.

Value set by reputations
And monumental possessions,
Materialistic confessions.

They prayed they would
See there's more to life than me.

Time is always the greatest
Construct, so slow,
So fast at times.

She took it for granted
While she discovered
Busta Rhymes
And
Afro curl.

He wouldn't mind
Going back to the times
A man was a boy.

Masculinity wasn't a
Requirement,
And toxic thoughts
Only existed in women.
Unfortunate, I say.

He must grow to be the wise,
To seek pure happiness
And hide the feel.

Only to find ten years down the line he's still the boy
In a delinquent
Mind.

She gasps for breath—gasp—

As she realises these

Common phases are
All surprises.

Don't

Don't be a man's fool.
It bears deep.

I'm sure you've found it.

Don't root it all;
It can't be counted.

Don't say a wish
And
Hope it drowns it.

Don't bring it near and seek around it.

Don't copy it
So it can bound it.

Don't be ashamed
You were surrounded.

Don't bare it all;
It can bring soundness.

Don't call on sisters
Who can't account
It.

Don't judge by looks
But how you found it.

Don't always sulk;
It brings great sadness.

Don't be afraid to know what
Love is.

Hey, I'm just a writer.
Don't take me.

I only write what I
Feel
Round it.

It works for me,
And
So I found it.

I hope it works for
You too.
Someday we'll only crown it.

Truth

She loves it.
It takes her away.
It breaches her soul.

It's only a matter of time.
They realise the eyes
Are not lies.

The soul can be unwoven
And shredded down to a
Single thread.

To only find that I
Is she,
And she is me.

The temptation,
The fears,
The concerns of time.

Don't linger around her
Because she's a star,
Destined for more than you
Ask for.

The delight in humble
Minds
Only trails.

I wish she'd seen the truth.

Sometimes it's easier to mind.

The magnitude of doubt
Sometimes too heavy for strength.

I wish she'd see the truth.

The air the young mind,
All so innocent and kind
To her.

So she sees the gloomy lights
And the compost
That they set aside,
And
If only she could see there's more to it
Than she.

She'd realise the eyes
Are not lies,
And it's been that way
For decades
So sincerely.

Section 3

Hate, it has caused a lot of problems in the world, but has not solved one yet.

~Maya Angelou

Birth

Those that are free
When they can be,
When they want to be.

A true black myth passed on by centuries
Of tearful eyes and dry cries.

Shackles, shackles—
Heavy. Painful. Painless.

Free like the wind,
Chained to the ground
So deep it lasts awhile.
Up until now. Nothing big, nothing
Important a day, a year.

Some choose to see and ignore.
So sad compassion at their door,
Too blinded by society's roar.

Some would say 'equality';
Others would say 'racism'.

Shackles, shackles—
Painless. Heavy. Painful.
Now once forgotten.

Black lives do and will always matter. There's no negotiation.

Warm

Your skin golden.
Your beauty solemn.

It could never be less
Bold
Than your mind evolving.

"You're precious," I tell
You.

Time may resolve,
But you're everlasting.

Those before you
Believed in you
Before you believed
In yourself.

Quit counting;
It's forever
Mount.

It's from the greatness.

From afro curl
And
Never denying.

Real beauty lies
Within.

So don't lose hope.

We'll work around it,
And
Make sure it's sounded.
Your skin golden,
Your beauty solemn,
And
Black is golden.

Hope

Roots so deep
And
Countless.

Seek the brightness
For souls are
Heavy and timeless.

Oh, dear mind,
Why do you cloud
Mess?

Years of growing,
You'd think we want
Less.

He didn't mind
This, whatever
Came next.

She'd hope the lightness
Would overcrowd mess,
And minds of richness
Would never seek less.

For souls are heavy
And
Timeless

In a world so righteous.

Kryptonite

Magical energy
Flows through you
Right.

I dare you to
Fight it.

You're out of this
World; don't
Hide it.

They'll gaze at
Your perplexity.

Now don't dare
Hide it.

It roots from ancestral bonds
Of joy
And
Likeness.

So pay attention
To the within,
And
Shine that light, pet.

You'll be amazed
At all
Its gleaming.

Section 4

Imagine your life is perfect in every respect; what would it look like?

~Brian Tracy

Free

It's all it is.
A picture of
This.

Life on pause
With a little
Grey list.

Only a day
She'd want to obey.

So frightful
Of all the things
They say!

It's never forthcoming.

Nights so undenying
And
Now so ongoing.

She'd take all it's
Founded.

Blah

Wonder if she may,
Always a day
Away.

If she could see it
Too.

The mist, the gloom,
And
All its blue.

She might sit down
Awhile
And
Enjoy the midnight fire.

For it forever goes
On
To its heart's
Desire.

Now we must
Intrude.
It's 1982.

It's really delightful
And
All so unspiteful.

I don't mind
The mere
Wind of it all.

It's never so frightening
Until you'll fight it.

I dare you to
Remind it.

The '80s were great aliveness.
And
Peaceful minds
Are more less
Doubtless.

Mare

I'm sure the adults
Don't know about
It,

Whatever's bringing
Doubt.
Pet.

They clean all sorrows;
How about that.
Pet.

They're not organised.
It's all great lies.
Pet.

They'd rather take
Someone else's light
Then
Work around it.

What a shame
They can't be counted
So little minds
Don't feel astounded.

The pressure's bait
For those who've
Been taken by it.

"I didn't ask for this."

Okay, well drown it.

Curse

It is I,
The one who calls for,
Sits for.

Waits for
That abandoned stare
I wish to dare.

Only to be aware
Of rooting despair.

I wish you'd dare
To see no mares.

Section 5

Start where you are. Use what you have. Do what you can.

~Arthur Ashe

Mode

The clock keeps,
The door creaks
In mode
And
Silence.

The many encounters
Day by day,
The hush.

The rush against
Time,
Against patience.

Bring them to the lands.

The time is not
Discreditable
And
Lasts.

The faces may
Worry less
And
Be met with no disgraces.

Myth

Those county lines
So thin,
So inclined.

Before it all
Were diamonds
And
Shore.

Even the seashells
Would soar
In all its awe.

The clouds
Would meet
And
Show defeat.

For they were
Commanders
Of the skies.

It may rain.
It may not.

The diamonds
Still glisten
Through the lot.

Dream

I guess the gates
Of rain

Will flood again,
And
The shepherds
Will say,

"What's that, dear friend?"

For they have
Never seen
So many souls
That do not gleam

In the atmosphere of
Dreams.

Light

Indeed you were
So small and
Brave.

You thought the
World was
Little and round.

It revolved around
You and all
You saw fit.

You'd dress yourself
And
Deem yourself a
Princess or prince.

Never did you feel
The weight of
Constant aches
From the adult state.

You admired it all.

The beauty of life.

You didn't think of
All that wasn't right.

Indeed, that was all right.

Until you become
An open shell
With puzzles to fill.

You no longer
Saw the light.

Near

Fear is all but
Near.

Like leeches it feeds.

All the suffering
It leads.

No man can lead.

The pain it leaves

So close to disease.

They've felt it breed
And
Watched it leave.

So many don't see.

Why is that?

The sorrows of all

They feel, not bold.
But
The earth will cry
Until it feels like gold.

Beauty

Flaunt this way,
And
You'll see the way
They stare and prey.

A women's beauty
Is key to solace.

Though some may
Say,

"She's just a woman",

Without noticing that
That's the beauty
Within them.

All from womb, no one
Can miss them.

About the Author

Carolyn Sabuni is London born and raised. She's a Sagittarius at heart if you're into star signs.

She always had a love for reading growing up, beginning with Jacqueline Wilson's books to *The Diary of a Wimpy Kid*, and many others.

She was part of a performing arts school for nine years which involved tap, ballet, and contemporary dance. She performed at the Royal Albert Hall.

You can contact her at the following:

Email: carolynsabuni45@gmail.com

Instagram: @csvoice_o

Printed in the United States
by Baker & Taylor Publisher Services